QUICK GUIDE & TIPS TO CHRISTIAN MUSIC
EXPOSE, PROMOTE, AND INCREASE YOUR MUSIC MINISTRY
by
Kellen "Cache" Coleman

Want to Thank God All Mighty for using a broken Vessel like myself to serve in his Kingdom. I will also thank my Wife who spent precious time reviewing and approving this book. Mucho Gracias to: Eric Leaman of ProlificMgmt, & Author D Michelle Thompson for reviewing, and editing. A sincere thank you to all the clients I have been allowed to serve in their ministries and build together 5ive, Norris J, Domingo Guyton, Horace Christian, Dwanye Jenkins, SeriousVoice, Kre8tor, Ken Ken, Elan Brio, the staff at the ICRS. Thank you to my Mom and Father Margie and Chris Thomas and my Entire Family. Also to all those media outlets and others in the industry that I don't have room to name all that reply and say yes and no and mentor me in this walk Tyrone Smith, Rick Greene, Jason Hollis, Chris Chicago, DeeJay Splash, the list goes on. And to my church family especially those who showed unconditional love in the most challenging time of my life and helped strengthen my marriage Pastor Bracken and Donna Christian and the whole Harvest Church in Lubbock.

ISBN 978-0-615-97545-0

Printed in the United States of America

Preface

In the past, I spent more than a decade working on secular music projects that never seemed to make the big bucks. Some made a splash, but most were lost and forgotten puddles. Few people even remembered them unless they knew me personally. I also taught parenting classes and life skills at the county jail in Lubbock, TX, and unfortunately put myself in a situation that landed me an overnight stay at that jail. I had become a resident of this $100 million dollar jail, with almost $100,000 worth of bail.

After experiencing this stay at the jail, I made the decision to fully commit myself to God, and turned my focus over to working with only Christian artists. When looking back on my life, I realized this was a long, overdue wake-up call. As seen in the scripture below, I was using my skills for the works of the devil, rather than the will of God. Once I committed my works to Christ, he was able to bless me in everything I do for him.

Psalm 1:1 KJV "Blessed is the man that walketh not in the counsel of the ungodly, nor standeth in the way of sinners, nor sitteth in the seat of the scornful"

I have worked in various areas of the entertainment industry. These experiences include magazines, newspapers, online radio, public relations, artist management, and web design. I have also traveled to multiple countries spanning three continents and attended multiple award shows, but not once had I thought I was called to use these experiences for Christ.

When serving, mentoring, and counseling fellow Christians, I have a couple of key biblical rules:

#1) We are all part of part of Christ's body and we should act like it
Romans 12:4-8 For just as each of us has one body with many members, and these members do not all have the same function, [5] so in Christ we, though many, form one body, and each member belongs to all the others.

We have to remember who we are serving. No matter what our CV or resume says, we are one thing, and that's a servant of The Most High. Servant hood is not a something you do while you are in transition trying to get to the next level but it is a life style. It is not a fad, not something you do while waiting for your real break. While in the church I have met a bunch of church goers who act like servants but really believe that servant hood is beneath them.

#2) Do not judge other believers' motives.

Philippians 1:15-18 KJV *"Some indeed preach Christ even of envy and strife; and some also of good will. [16] The one preach Christ of contention, not sincerely, supposing to add affliction to my bonds. [17] But the other of love, knowing that I am set for the defence of the gospel [18] What then? notwithstanding, every way, whether in pretence, or in truth, Christ is preached; and I therein do rejoice, yea, and will rejoice.*

When working with artists, we have a clear understanding that we do not judge other artists or speak negatively about them. There will always be disagreements with how others conduct themselves, but we must know that God works in mysterious ways. We may never understand the reasons for those situations, but I will support others as long as they are working for Christ. This is very important for artists to know about me so that they comprehend my motives when working with them. It's not that I think they are any greater or lesser than any of my other clients. I am here for Christ, and I am working with them because they are serving Christ as well, not their own selfish desires. I do not judge others, but there have been acts that I have separated myself from because the Holy Spirit within me directed me to. I choose not to serve certain artist anymore once it became clear they are not committed to serving God with unselfish motives.

Chapter 1: Ask Yourself "Why Am I Doing Music?"

Why am I doing music? This is the first question that you should ask yourself as a Christian musician before you record one song, shoot one video, or step on any stage to perform. For your vision or goal to flourish, your motivation must be pure. Answering the question initially will save you some heartache and stress later when the going gets tough.

Matthew 22:14 (KJV) "For many are called, but few are chosen."

I strongly believe that what separates the people being called from the people that are chosen is the way in which they respond. Remember that many artists will hear the call of God, but few will respond. Jesus said many times "He who has ears to hear, let him hear" (Matthew 11:15; Mark 4:9; Luke 8:8, 14:35). The point is that everyone has ears, but only a few are listening and responding.

Listening is an art form that is almost lost in today's society and most people have trouble listening in the physical sense which is entirely different from listening to the Holy Spirit. In today's microwave mentality (the everything now mentality) we are flooded with so much information all the time. Things are always screaming for our attention and this is exactly opposite from the way that the Holy Spirit works. The Holy Spirit is a gentleman and will not impose his will on yours. To hear from the Holy Spirit you need to unclutter your spiritual ears.

Every other Christian artist I meet say that they want to use their music to minister to people, and that God has called them to do that. God calls us all and when he does he will give us a vision. However often times people veer from the original vision because they sometimes stop listening to the Holy Spirit, revise the vision because they start putting their own remix on God's plan, or quite frankly rewrite the vision because they believe they can help God with the vision for their lives. Nowadays, everyone is an expert at something and everyone is a life coach and motivational speaker. I have often thought to myself, the number of life coaches and experts have increased exponentially in society however society is becoming more depraved and alarmingly jaded. Maybe just maybe these coaches are training people for the wrong team. Hint hint Christians rise up and fulfill the great commission (Matthew 28:19) which is to make disciples of all nations. If God calls you to reach people through your music, your daily life must reflect the character of God. You can't claim to be a Christian musician waiting for your big break and you haven't even shared the word with anyone in a year. The point here is we have a responsibility to make disciples of all nations and they best way to make disciples is by living an exemplary life. Yes Jesus preached to the crowds but he didn't regard the masses as disciples. His disciples were a few that he handpicked personally.

Our mission is simple as seen in Matthew 28:19:

(KJV) "Therefore, and teach all nations, baptizing them in the name of the Father, and of the Son, and of the Holy Ghost"

(NIV) "Therefore go and make disciples of all nations, baptizing them in the name of the Father and of the Son and of the Holy Spirit."

There have been artists who never thought of getting paid, but have been blessed to do this full time. So have a pure heart for doing Christian music, because IT IS MINISTRY FIRST, AND MUSIC SECOND. Even if you don't sell one song, or nobody applauds you, you should still impact people's lives by sharing the Word of God, which is the Holy Bible. Money comes for some, but there will be others that never get paid. Your anointing is a spiritual thing and blessings are not entirely financial.

I have personally met Christian artist that profess that they want to be the next Beiber, Beyonce or Lil Wayne and that shocks me because they are using worldly standards of success to define a vision that they supposedly got from God. Now do not misunderstand me but I firmly believe that Christian artist can be and should be just as financially successful as any of the artist that I mentioned above however, I do not believe that we should let the world set the standards for our success. You cannot have a hidden agenda with the most high and not being honest with yourself about your motives doesn't hurt God, it only hurts you. Trust me the devil will try to use your real motives to destroy you.

Paul tells us in Corinthians to check ourselves now maybe he doesn't say it in today's vernacular but the point is we must continuously examine our hearts. (2 Corinthians 13:5) Your heart could lead you astray, this is clearly evident in today's culture of divorce. People change their hearts on a whim and don't seem to want to take responsibilities for their own actions.

2 Corinthians 13:5 (MSG) Test yourselves to make sure you are solid in the faith. Don't drift along taking everything for granted. Give yourselves regular checkups. You need firsthand evidence, not mere hearsay, that Jesus Christ is in you. Test it out. If you fail the test, do something about it.

We aren't here to make money, we are here to bring folks to Christ. That should be the main reason a Christian artist should get into music ministry. However if you want to have a chance at making money, here are a couple things that the most successful Christian artists have in common:

1) First of all, they write down a mission statement and goals. Write down a mission statement and the work that you believe God has called you to do. The reason you do this is because if you ever wander off trail, you have something that is documented to remind you what the original vision was. Know that once finances get involved in your music ministry, things will get complicated. Your mission can get jaded due to the lack of money coming in, or even with an abundance of money coming in.

2) They are active member in their church. They are not just members, but active members getting involved in more than just making music. A lot of them will take on leadership roles in other areas including intercession, children's or youth ministry and outreach ministry just to name a few.

3. They have a family, and spend time with them. You have to be a leader in your own home. Don't try to do mission trips in Haiti and Africa while most people in your family have no idea that you are living for Christ.

Chapter 2: Getting Started and Setting Up Your Ministry Business

You are first an artist, so music and creation may come easy to you. You have studied, and even more often played around, before you made the decision to answer THE CALL to do this for God. There is also another hat you need to wear, and that's business man or woman. Even if you don't make a dime, or plan to ever sell your music, you should structure your craft as a business. This is necessary in case you change your mind, or find an opportunity to work for, or become, a non-profit organization. The first step in every organization is foundation, planning, and goal setting (FPG). Keep all receipts for equipment bought, or any other expense incurred from doing music. It's easy to do this by buying a portable scanner, which is now less than $100 in some stores. The receipts scan right into the computer, and you can gather your costs to send quarterly and/or annually to a qualified CPA.

Every organization should know their budget. The purpose isn't to limit yourself, but it enables you to know what you are able to do with your current financial status. However, never forget the supernatural is what we believe in, and your budget can increase in a second, when God opens a new door supernaturally. Most people have no idea what to do with a $5, or even a five million dollar budget. After faithfully watching The Shark Tank, I learned that a leader of an organization should always know their numbers. If you don't know your numbers, you can look and sound like an ignorant idiot.

Even more important than a budget, you need a business license or DBA (Doing Business as Sole Proprietorship). This license is free in many cities, and is enough to get you off the ground. Few artists may want to go non-profit, which we will cover in later chapters. Get a business license whether you plan on selling or not, because if you are caught selling music on the street, online, or at a flea market, you could be in violation of a law that you aren't aware of. Getting a license will have you legal as a Christian artist.

Artists often ask how to find other Christian artists and producers. I recommend CHRISTIANSTAR.ME because it is a beneficial website. I recommend this site to those in all areas of the business for networking, mentoring, and working with each other. Now I must make a disclosure here I own and operate the CHRISTIANSTAR.ME website. I think that it is beneficial for people that want to get their music out in a place where other musicians can get to listen and appreciate their style. Also a lot of collaborations have been engendered by this website. You can also ask fellow church members, especially those in the choir and band. Musicians know musicians, and they could lead you to some legitimate connections. Remember, a closed mouth doesn't get fed. There is a youth group in almost every region of the country that has at least one awesome music ministry. Networking with others at Christian events is invaluable, especially those that have energetic young people.

Every musician should study music for about one year before releasing an album in the natural. This will allow the artists to record, learn at workshops, travel and fellowship with other musicians. During this time, allow the more mature artists to listen to your music, and find a mentor to help you along the journey. Many artists think that if they get a feature from a big-name artists they will get to become famous, but they quickly find this to be untrue. Unless it's a feature with the top star at the moment the chances of you getting famous from a feature are slim to none. You must keep in mind that stars cost money at least more than any average artist can afford. Also a star is going to make sure you have their money upfront and sign an agreement that you market the song properly which requires large sums of money that most debuting artists cannot afford.

Chapter 3: Financing Your Project in the Beginning

Before agreeing to represent any client, I ask them to set a budget and show me how much they have available to spend on promotion and publicity. Many artists have no idea on what their limitations are, which is a scary given that most start with a budget of less than a thousand dollars. I do this not because I want to spend their entire budget, but so that they can recognize and correct their ignorance about the business aspect. See, when a client comes to me, that usually means they want to increase their audience outside of their church, community, city, state, and often the country as well. If an artist has no money budgeted to buy advertising, travel, CD's, studio time, or a website, it's not a project that I want to be a part of because we are very limited in what we can actually do. Now it doesn't have to be a big budget and it will vary with each individual artists and their unique situation.

To pay for initial fees, I tell artists to make a goal of selling 6 CD's per day "on the street". The reason is, if an artists sets out to sell 6 CD's per day, the cost of producing those CD's can be as low as $1.56, including shipping costs. If an artist sells 6 of them at $10 each, he profits $8.44 each. This is a gross margin of 84.40%, and not too many businesses can get that much profit with products manufactured and purchased in the United States. Selling those 6 CD's per day would be a profit of $50.64 per day, which would be a total profit of $1519.20 per month.

Often artists complain in frustration about how much money they don't have, but what if you took two hrs per day to reach this goal? I have seen untalented secular artists sell more than 6 CD's per day in less than a two hour time period. They used aggressive and persuasive sales tactics because they were desperate to make a living. I know if God has truly called a Christian artist, they can surpass anyone in the secular with FAITH. Now, it's very important that the artists avoid the BIG HEAD, which is a whole other chapter in this book. Instead, think about this $1519.20 monthly increase in their ministry, and how they can start to live off it. You may be able to buy yourself new equipment, or pay a company cell phone bill that you will later claim on taxes. However, you won't be able to live off of this money. You will be able to pay for a publicist, radio, and video promoter, web developer, and website ads that can all escalate you to the next level.

The next important part about music ministry as aforementioned is knowing your numbers, like with any business you are trying to make a profit from. I have met very few artists who truly know their numbers, which is crucial if you ever want to get into massive retail. The distributor should not be the only one who knows the profit margins. The artists should maintain accurate records for IRS purposes, business purposes, and most importantly tithing purposes.

2 Corinthians 9:6-15 "6 Whoever sows sparingly will also reap sparingly, and whoever sows generously will also reap generously. 7 Each man should give what he has decided in his heart to give, not reluctantly or under compulsion, for God loves a cheerful giver. 8 And God is able to make all grace abound to you, so that in all things at all times, having all that you need, you will abound in every good work. 9 He has scattered abroad his gifts to the poor; his righteousness endures forever. 10 Now he who supplies seed to the sower and bread for food will also supply and increase your store of seed and will enlarge the harvest of your righteousness. 11 You will be made rich in every way so that you can be generous on every occasion, and through us your generosity will result in thanksgiving to God. 12 This service that you perform is not only supplying the needs of God's people but is also overflowing in many expressions of thanks to God. 13 Because of the service by which you have proved yourselves, men will praise God for the obedience that accompanies your confession of the gospel of Christ, and for your generosity in sharing with them and with everyone else. 14 And in their prayers for you their hearts will go out to you, because of the surpassing grace God has given you. 15 Thanks be to God for his indescribable gift!

Galatians 6:7 Do not be deceived: God is not mocked, for whatever one sows, that will he also reap.

The Bible is full of parables and teachings on sowing, but so many ministries decide to only sow into their own ministry. I have seen 100% fail rate in all music ministries that do not practice the biblical principle of sowing. Most of the time, these epic failures are not even speckled with small increases.

Chapter 4 Public Relations

This will probably be my easiest chapter to write, because I have had over a decade of experience in public relations. From finishing a Master Degree program in communication, to using the skills in the real world that schools can't teach, I have helped various clients in both the secular and Christian realm of music, movies, magazines, radio, small businesses from trucking, non-profits and the list goes on. I have held the title of Communications Intern in Washington D.C. for Congress Woman Yvette D. Clarke representing Brooklyn, NY. I have also worked with State Representative Benjamin Swan in Springfield, Massachusetts. My experience is vast in media and it all started from getting paid in CD's and creating a value for my services. Typically I don't like following the typical PR rules because I believe every project is unique therefore instead of working with a company that wants you to follow a cookie cutter model I love to be contracted and work independently with the organization.

Public Relations is a mix of writing press releases contacting media, giving your opinion going into the consulting arena and I love every minute of it. It typically is a position for those who love getting people into the spotlight without ever having to be in it. Many publicists believe all press is good press because at least people are talking about you. I completely disagree because this shows a lack of discipline on the part of the artist and ineffectiveness on the part of the publicist; two things that I do not want to be associated with. That being said, you cannot control people and the things that they do or say and as such sometimes there are mistakes that are made that have to be cleaned up. In the more recent years people think they can wake up one day and become a publicist, that's true you can call yourself whatever you wish but are you effective?

An effective publicist can write, evaluate the new trends in the industry they are in, get the product out to the networks which are more than media, but even bloggers and everyday people. I always enjoyed PR because it allows a person to present instead of sell, a salesman gets commission off what they sell. A publicist gets paid upfront for what they will present. This chapter is not about me it's about how PR works and how to pick a publicist. If you decide to go with an established publicist avoid anybody who guarantees any fame, this is entertainment nobody can guarantee anything. What can be guaranteed is the publicist will provide proof of coverage in magazines, and some can record or get the audio for radio interviews and film clips for television. Even though all that can be done understand if you are paying a discount price you will get what you pay for. Publicists are limited by their budget even though they can get creative; they can't always do all that the client needs if the customer isn't willing to pay the full price.

Word of advice, always ask the publicist's price for full time and part time and how much the different services cost. Ask the publicist for a track record because most established publicists have a portfolio on their website and their repertoire of clients they have can show you what the publicist has accomplished. If you choose to give a rookie a chance ask them if they have studied the particular genre you are in and detail how they will obtain interviews and plan to accomplish what they are selling to you. Publicists are marketers and presenters and the great ones are effective communicators with everybody that crosses their path.

Chapter 5: To Sell, Or Not To Sell - Profit vs. Non-Profit

The decision to sell, or not to sell your music, is something you have to go in prayer for and ask God what he wants you to do. All artists would love to give their music away for free so that the whole world could hear it without having the burden of selling it. This will not be a reality for the majority of Christian artists, but still many try to sell their music until they find someone who says they can't afford it. Then they end up giving away hundreds, if not thousands of dollars worth of CD's. I tell artists who decide to sell their music, to not give any CD's away for free. Instead, I advise them that if they find someone who can't afford it or isn't willing to pay, just give them a business card that has their name, and most importantly their website where they can download the artist's free mixtape. Since most mixtapes have other people's beats on them and legally can't be sold, it's a win-win for both.

The future customer becomes a fan first, and gets free music in the process. Suppose that an artist meets 1000 people who are unable to pay for their music. The artist is able to save money by not giving a $1.56 CD away to a thousand people, which would cost $1560.00 Instead they are giving away a .35 cent business card to a thousand people which would cost $35. Either item could be expensed on your taxes, but the first free item could break your business while the other is affordable on a reasonable budget.

Some think that because they are doing God's business, they have to go non-profit. I am not one of those who believe you have to. Some are called to do more than just music. They may use their music as a stepping stone to create their own group home, or residential treatment center. In this case it may benefit them to go non-profit, but many won't go through the extensive process it takes to set this up. There are a lot of rules to non-profits, and if you make a mistake, it can cost you not just a lot of money, but time and headaches as well.

Chapter 6: How to Market, and With Whom

As mentioned in previous chapters, Christian artists should be working with other Christians who have dedicated themselves to Christ. Since there is a God, there is also a devil. There are different spirits, both good and bad. Music is a powerful tool that has influenced people to change their lives and follow Christ, We also hear of demonic spirits that have told people through music to kill others, commit suicide, and more. If that is true, it's very possible that working with someone who creates music for the devil can have an influence on Christian music. There is a satanic movement in Christian music that has more and more artists taking God or Jesus out of their message. They are looking for that crossover hit in order to make the Billboards, Grammies, etc.

Yes, we are to minister to the lost, but we are supposed to bring them into the light, not be like them. We aren't perfect, but we are forgiven. The worldly artists have transformed more Christian artists than Christian artists have transformed the world's. In saying all that, we should have Christian producers, promoters, labels, distribution, and more. Shamrock Media operated by Chris Chicago is a great avenue, especially in Rock and Rap. They do honest, effective business, and have been successful with number one hits for over a decade. Another endorsement is Infinity Distribution, which is part of Central South. This is also an honest and effective business run by great teachers Rick Greene and Jason Hollis. These are just a few examples of Christians in the market place.

The best marketing is by word of mouth, marketing at school and work, and doing street ministry. It's not what you do, it's who you are. Let your light shine everywhere you go. It's not that you should brag, but you should be letting folks know about your light, the word, and your God.

Chapter 7 Christian Radio

There are over 200 outlets that play Christian radio in this country alone, and it is up to the artists or their publicist to find them. Later in this book, we will share a very detailed media list. Internet radio is the easiest type of radio to get on, because many of these stations don't have to worry about advertisement dollars. Many internet radio stations are run right from home, and their only costs are time, equipment, domain hosting, and electricity. Internet radio doesn't have to follow FCC regulations or pay their fees, marketing, staff, lights, etc. Just because Internet radio doesn't have a massive overhead doesn't mean you can't support them financially. The more you finance Internet radio stations, the greater they grow. FM/AM radio stations cost thousands, or even millions of dollars to operate. They have to think more corporate than independent, unlike the internet stations that think independent. Many of us love thinking independent more than corporate, because corporations require money to set up. Money that most people will never earn, even after a lifetime in the business.

Christian radio is good, but also remember that stations have formats. If you don't fit their format, just move on to the next. This next sentence is controversial and hopefully will change, but some stations have shown ignorance and bigotry by playing rock/rap songs that are good songs, but deny true Christian rappers a spot. Now this is not just a white vs. black thing. Don't get confused, even some black stations that are power players (especially in the south) have denied playing major Black Christian rap artists without a legal form of payola. They sometimes want the top Christian rapper of the time to pay $20,000 just to get into the Atlanta market. I could name drop and go into details that I have seen and heard but I don't think it would help.

So whether it's a major Christian station that will play a white rocker/rapper, but not a black one, or a station that will only play Black Gospel who has paid for the airtime, the division has to stop. If it's ministry first, and if it's about impacting and helping to save souls, this division must stop. If you think it's about format, faith, religion, tradition, and money before ministry, then please stop reading my book right now and spend some time in the word. I believe the bible when it says:

Romans 12:6-8 (NKJV) "Having then gifts differing according to the grace that is given to us, let us use them: if prophecy, let us prophesy in proportion to our faith; [7] *or ministry, let us use it in our ministering; he who teaches, in teaching;* [8] *he who exhorts, in exhortation; he who gives, with liberality; he who leads, with diligence; he who shows mercy, with cheerfulness".*

The facts are, you are NOT going to be accepted by every radio outlet, and that is ok. What you must do though, is be diligent in submitting your music to radio. You must make sure your press release is well written, and that your songs are titled properly. Make sure the files are sent to the station the way they prefer, whether it's in the body of an email, or sent as attachments. Done are the days of massive email list and copy and pasting galore. At least 50% of the most popular sites don't accept those emails and probably like me ignore them, send them to spam or just delete them. Contacting radio is like contacting a potential date. You must personalize it, and read the instructions on the website so that you submit them properly. Some sites will not download at all because of all of the viruses out there. Make sure you know your target so you can give them what they require.

Chapter 8 Preparation For The Next Level

Every ministry business and individual wants to move to the next level. The Bible tells us we are to be the head and not the tail, so this desire is biblical and natural. For Christian ministries, we must be careful to evaluate what that "NEXT LEVEL" is. We must make sure we are clear that we are running our own race, and not get caught up in the sensationalism of the entertainment side. Do not get caught up in comparing our level to anybody else's level and accomplishments. Comparing yourself with others can cripple a ministry, and can really stunt growth. The next level for one ministry may be doing ten more shows a year, and for another ministry it's doing interviews with the media from all over the world. Few ministries will reach the level of national or international popularity, and that's not necessarily a bad thing. Charity starts at home, and before you minister out of state, you should be ministering in your home state, your local churches, and your own home. Often young men, especially newly saved, say God has called them to minister at the national or international level meanwhile their homes are in chaos. This is a contradiction of the scriptures, and it is not God's will. We know that God is not a God of confusion, and it's confusing to have people see a minister in church praising God, but at home they are cheating and beating on their spouse, or not taking care of their children.

It has been said that preparation makes you ready when an opportunity is available. You need to be ready for the next level, whatever that is for you. Your house must be in order, just as we all need to be ready for Christ's return. Too often ministries don't have their affairs in order, from financial statements to merchandise orders, to a list of past and future shows. Ministry is not a business, its ministry.

However, it is similar to a business in the sense that you must keep good records, maintain relationships, and always keep reliability a priority As Christ's disciples; we should have order in our lives. So when preparing your quest for the next level, make sure you prep, plan, and document your progress. Write everything down in order, as if you were writing a "How To" manual. Every successful business has a manual so that all new employees have a guideline to follow. This allows everybody to be in one accord and doing the same thing, with the same information on how the organization operates.

The other part of the next level goes back to a previous chapter. Why are you doing this if you're whole goal is to be a superstar? Do it to let Christ shine instead of your personal ego or agenda. Too many Christian ministers are compromising with the world by taking God's word out, not wanting to say Jesus, and sinning in various ways. God won't bless that! In fact, his word actually says he will curse it, and you won't be known in the book of life. So if you do achieve the success that very few have received in Christian rap, make sure you don't gain the world and lose your soul. Make sure you don't gain all of the treasures of this world and miss out on the treasure in heaven. I say all of this in love and even these next comments are in love. I say them like an original gangster warns somebody not to step on his toes, and say "DON'T TRY TO PIMP GOD". Meaning don't try to get rich off his word. Many try this because they couldn't make it anymore in the world, because you have to be ruthless, cutthroat, and sharp as a blade. They come over to Christ and try to use their charm and talents just for riches.

<u>Chapter Media List</u>

Now, I understand this chapter may be the only reason you downloaded or bought this book. However, let me warn you that just having this information does not bless you. This list can help you expand your ministry, but be forewarned that it can destroy you as well. Let me explain a little further. Some people are right where they need to be. The reason you aren't getting airplay, distribution, or massive shows is from lack of faith, talent, or purpose. This list is shared because I think the information was given to me from God. The multiple hours that it took to put the contacts together were not of me, but it was by the talents that God gave me to collect it. In the world they would never share this type of information in fear of losing money. Since this is MINISTRY FIRST, we as Christians shouldn't have those worries, especially if we believe...

Jer 29:11 (NIV) "For I know the plans I have for you," declares the Lord, "plans to prosper you and not to harm you, plans to give you hope and a future."

This list can destroy you because it can expose you. Some were not called to this and are being called to another position in the Kingdom, but won't obey. It can destroy you because you can spend twelve months sending a quality track that is missing God's power, and get zero to few responses from these contacts. Remember what this message says...

1 Cor 12 "It's not all apostle, not all Prophet, not all miracle worker, not all healer, not all prayer in tongues, not all interpreter of tongues, and yet some of you keep competing for so-called important parts".

I pray that this list inspires and helps ministries that may have never met me, or a person like me. I pray that this message shows love within the community, and a willingness to work together. I pray this media list blesses a ministry that wouldn't have the finances to pay someone else to send thousands of emails out. Lastly, I pray that this list is a blessing, and that others will follow and share the information.

CHRISTIANSTAR.ME MEDIA LIST

Distribution
http://www.distribber.com/story
http://www.centralsouthdistribution.com/news.php?viewStory=112
http://www.infinitymusicdistribution.com
http://breathecast.christianpost.com
http://www.indiebible.com/icb/musicdistributionarticle.shtml
http://www.wesscottmarketing.com Films
http://www.newdaychristian.com/ music and books

Christian Night Clubs
Springfield, MA http://www.gospelbeat.org/
Minnesota Christian night clubs http://www.3degreesministries.com
 Minnesota http://www.northstarroom.org/
Club IOU doge city MN, facebook only
Club Jesus Oakland, CA AT Word Assembly last Friday of each month.
 http://www.wordassemblychurch.org

AWARD SHOWS
Dove Awards www.doveawards.com
Stellar Awardshttp://www.thestellarawards.com
 EnSoundmusicawards   http://www.ensoundmusicawards.org
African Gospel Awardshttp://africagospelawards.com/
http://www.therhythmofgospelawards.com

Christian Magazines
http://uccmag.com/a-chat-with-tru-praise/ new york
http://www.inhistepsmag.org/ African Christian Mag Nigeria, ZA,
Nambia

www.ccmmagazine.com
Gospel magazinehttp://mygospeltoday.com
http://www.empower-magazine.com
http://guerillacross.com/home/?page_id=80
Speak Life Online radio show every Tuesday 7pm-9pm on
guerillacross.com
http://insidegospelonline.com/#
http://www.blogmagazine.org
http://www.thesoulmag.com/
http://www.descalate.com/the-commissioned-magazine.html
http://www.totalprayze.com/encore/

Christian websites
www.urbanmediaga.com
www.trinity103atl.com
http://www.power104atl.com/ **Atlanta**
http://www.blogtalkradio.com/niacom **Dallas online Michael**
Johnson
http://www.victory1075.com/Sound-Doctrine.html **Kendal online**
http://www.thegospeltribuneatlanta.com/gta-radio/ **Atlanta**
http://www.gospelcitynaija.com **Niaja**
http://www.modernghana.com/ **Ghana**
http://studio6naija.com/ **Nigeria**
korrectnation.com **Nigeria**
http://gospelmusicnaija.com/ **Nigeria**
http://www.rapzilla.com
http://www.hhhdb.com
http://community.loudcity.com/stations/altared-lives-radio/files/show/
http://www.sphereofhiphop.com
http://www.gospelpundit.com

http://www.gospelreggae.com/
http://www.dasouth.com
http://preachpastor.com
https://www.watchimpact.com
Website owned by Actor Kirk Cameron from FireProof
http://www.worldmag.com
http://westcoastfiya.com/
http://www.acmpmediagroup.com
http://thegospelguru.com/
http://samixtapes.wordpress.com/
http://www.christiankick.com/

Christian film makers
http://www.echolight.com/info/about.php

Gospel TV show
http://www.tbn.co.za/tv-guide TBN AFRICA
http://thegripshow.com/ TBN AFRICA
 RightNowOnTV.com
http://www.skyangel.com
http://goodnews20-4.tv Dallas
http://www.mygoodnewstv.com/ Phoenix
http://www.harvest-tv.com Indiana
http://lifetoday.org/contact/
http://spirit-television.com
http://www.nrbnetwork.tv/
http://parables.tv
Pureflix.com
http://www.uptv.com **Uplifting Entertainment 51mil viewers**
http://www.god.tv/businessangel

http://3abn.org/
http://www.godslearningchannel.com **Midland**
http://www.theangelsnetwork.org/
Daystar.com
http://www.jctv.org/flashindex.php
 http://www2.crossroads.ca/fullcircle/
http://crossroads.ca/television/huntley
http://www.bostonpraiseradio.tv/
http://holyculture.net/
http://www.ohtv.co.uk Open Heaven OH TV, Magazine etc

TV show in Europe and Africa
http://www.sporah.com
http://holyhiphop.org/
http://christianhiphop.com
http://www.dagospeltruth.com

Great Website to Learn More about Music
http://www.praverb.net/

Gospel Publicist and Radio/TV promoters
Kellen Cache www.Christianstar.me
Rahru R. Arceneaux
http://rahru1.wix.com/hautechoclatmultimediagroup
Chris Chicago ShamrockMedia.com
Jason Hardy http://www.themprint.com/jhardyagency/
Frankie Wilson Gospel Media Content company
http://www.visionmedia1.com/
Cheryl Patterson http://universalxperience.wordpress.com
http://www.totalprayze.com/

<u>Christian retail events</u>
http://www.christianretailshow.com/

<u>Christian Association organization</u>
http://cbaonline.org/
http://www.twrafrica.org
http://www.twr.org
http://www.texasgag.com/

<u>Christian Festivals</u>
http://christianretailshow.com/
http://impactmovement.org/national-conference/
http://theextremetour.com/site/f-a-q/
http://www.easterfest.com
http://www.atlantafest.com/
http://sonshinefestival.com/
http://www.kingdombound.org/festival_tickets.php
http://www.jesusfestwv.org/
http://www.rockthedesert.com/
http://www.creationfest.com/
http://www.kingsfestival.com/
http://www.flavorfest.org/
http://www.cityofchicago.org/city/en/depts/dca/supp_info/chicago_gosp
el_musicfestival.html

<u>Christian Non Profits</u>
http://www.alleyesonmeinc.com

<u>Christian Comedians</u>
http://www.jredlive.com/
www.comedian**mikegoodwin**.com

<u>Christian Mixtape DJ'S</u>
http://djirockjesus.com/smh/?page_id=2283
http://southerngospelpraise.com/artists.htm

http://www.urband.org Pastor Urban D

http://www.urbancoachingnetwork.com

http://www.bigisthenewsmall.com/

Christian Radio
http://urbanfamilytalk.com 98.3FM WDFX Cleveland, MS
90.5FM WQVI Madison, MS
91.7FM WAJS Tupelo, MS
91.5FM WJGS Norwood, GA
http://kunm.org/programs/train-glory Alb New Mexico,sante fe, Las
vegas AM/FM
   http://breatheliferadio.com   Vacaville, CA
http://whcr.org/ New York Harlem
http://www.thehot1039.com Wichita Falls, TX
spiritco1.com Internet only
http://www.inspiration1390.com Chicago
http://www.hallelujah1600.com/main.html st louis
 Sunny 88.7 fm email jjdanquah@gmail.com
http://freedemradio.com/song-submission/
http://www.thegospelshow.com http://www.c895.org/schedule/
SEATTLE
1440 AM WDRJ Detroit
http://www.crown.edu/crown-radio DeeJay Splash
www.kbijr.us
http://www.churchbeatradio.com
http://www.cpopchristianmusic.com/
http://currentfm.com
http://www.mystaticradio.com Albuquerque, New Mexico
http://thepulseradio.net/
http://myk104.com/common/page.php?pt=streetswagg&id=75
http://mysunnyfmlive.com/content/presenters GH Host Jennifer of radio
http://www.ilovejccafe.com Ghana Host J. Smoke XFM
Philly radio station http://kbijr.us
http://www.kickinjamzradio.com

http://rejoice1110.com/index.html
http://www.dcnowradio.com/
http://www.thegospelsdj.com Fishbowl DJ Gabriel
http://www.tentalentsministry.com/ Fishbowl Dj Charles and Michelle
http://www.voiceofafricaradio.com London radio station
http://www.kingfmradio.com
http://www.gospelmusic.org/
http://love860.com/ Atlanta Christian radio station?
 http://yeslordradio.com/ylradio-urban.php

http://mypraiseatl.com/ Atl 102.5FM
http://www.donnieradio.com/ Donnie McClurkin
http://www.radiowinchcombe.co.uk/   Uk Gospel Radio
http://praisehouston.com Houston, TX
http://www.z180radio.com PLAYS RAP
http://www.ngenradio.com/ : Bay City 89.5 FM, Brenham 89.7 FM,
College Station 93.3 FM, Lake Jackson / Galveston 91.1 FM, Sugar
Land 99.5 FM, Houston / Humble 89.3 HD-2, Navasota 92.5 HD-2,

KNTU 88.1 FM 39.4 mi Mckinney, *TX*

KEOM 88.5 FM 9.2 mi   Mesquite, *TX*

KBEM 88.5 FM 4.5 mi   Minneapolis, MN

KCMP 89.3 FM 21.3 mi Northfield, MN

http://michiganchristianrapshows.blogspot.com/p/radio-station-
directory.html
http://www.rhemacentralcoast.com.au Aussie radio Plays Christian rap
and more
http://www.positivehits.com.au Aussie radio & TV
http://whoaradio.weebly.com/
http://www.krosswerdz.com radio and rappers
http://www.definitionradio.com Aussie radio

http://wadeoradio.com
http://jamthecity.com
http://www.cpopchristianmusic.com/
http://www.northlandradio1.com Michigan online r
http://www.joy97.com
http://www.sphereofhiphop.com

http://www.crossrap.com/christian-rap-artist-directory.html

http://www.praise963.com Knoxville, TX

Praise969.com North Augusta , SC

http://star1310.com Virginia Beach, VA

http://www.sgnthelight.com
radio stations that play Christian rap
http://michiganchristianrapshows.blogspot.com/p/radio-station-directory.html
http://www.myfusefm.com/?page_id=2
http://www.xfm951.com/
http://www.khvnam.com/ Dallas
http://www.gospelimpactradio.com
http://www.kggram.com/ Dallas Texas 1040am and 102.5fm
http://www.kwwj.org/home
http://www.kchl.org
http://www.kzzbradio.org KZZB-990AM Beaumont TX
http://www.koka.am/ Shreveport, LA

Radio Only

State	City	Station	Genre
Texas	Dallas/Ft. Worth	KGGR-1040AM	Urban Gospel
Texas	Dallas/Ft. Worth	KHVN-970AM	Urban Gospel
Texas	Dallas/Ft. Worth	KBFB-97.9FM	Mainstream Urban
Texas	Dallas/Ft. Worth	KKDA-104.5FM	Mainstream Urban
Texas	Dallas/Ft. Worth	KRNB-105.7FM	Urban AC
Texas	Houston	KYOK-1140AM	Urban Gospel
Texas	Houston	KWWJ-1360AM	Urban Gospel
Texas	Houston	KBXX-97.9	Mainstream Urban
Texas	Houston	KMJQ-102.1	Urban AC
Texas	Houston	KROI-92.1	Urban Gospel
Texas	San Antonio	KCHL-1480AM	Urban Gospel
Texas	Austin	KFIT-1060AM	Urban Gospel
Texas	Beaumont	KZZB-990AM	Urban Gospel
Texas	Killeen/Temple	KRMY-1050AM	Urban Gospel
Texas	Killeen/Temple	KIIZ-92.3FM	Mainstream Urban
Texas	Jacksonville	KJTX-104.5FM	Urban Gospel
California	Los Angeles	KJLH-102.3FM	Urban Contemp
California	Los Angeles	KTYM-1460AM	Urban Cont Gosp

State	Market	Station	Format
California	San Fransisco	KDYA-1190AM	Urban Gospel
California	San Fransisco	KMEL-106.1FM	Urban Contemp
California	San Diego	XHRM-92.5FM	Urban AC
California	Sacramento	KDEE-97.7FM	Urban AC
California	Stockton	KWIN-98.3FM	Urban Contemp
District of Colum	Washington	WYCB-1340AM	Urban Gospel
District of Colum	Washington	KPRS-104.1FM	Urban Gospel
District of Colum	Washington	WKYS-93.9FM	Mainstream Urban
District of Colum	Washington	WHUR-96.3FM	Urban AC
District of Colum	Washington	WMMJ-102.3FM	Urban AC
District of Colum	Washington	WPGC-95.5FM	Mainstream Urban
Florida	Miami/Ft.Lauderdale	WMBM-1490AM	Urban Gospel
Florida	Miami/Ft.Lauderdale	WEDR-99.0FM	Mainstream Urban
Florida	Miami/Ft.Lauderdale	WHQT-105.0FM	Urban AC
Florida	Tampa Bay	WRXB-1590AM	Urban Gospel
Florida	Tampa Bay	WBTP-95.7FM	Urban Contemp
Florida	Orlando/Daytona	WOKB-1680AM	Urban Gospel
Florida	Orlando/Daytona	WRMQ-1140AM	Urban Gospel

Florida	Orlando/Daytona	WCFB-94.9FM	Urban AC
Florida	Orlando/Daytona	WJHM-102.0FM	Mainstream Urban
Florida	Jacksonville	WZAZ-1400AM	Urban Gospel
Florida	Jacksonville	WJBT-93.3FM	Mainstream Urban
Florida	Jacksonville	WSOL-101.5FM	Urban AC
Florida	Jacksonville	WCGL-1360AM	Urban Gospel
Florida	Jacksonville	WFJO-92.5FM	Urban Gospel
Florida	West Palm Beach	WHFS-106.3FM	Urban AC
Florida	Pensacola	WRNE-980AM	Urban AC
Florida	Pensacola	WNVY-1090AM	Urban Gospel
Florida	Pensacola	WRRX-106.1FM	Urban AC
Florida	Tallahassee	WHBX-96.1FM	Urban AC
Florida	Tallahassee	WWLD-102.3FM	Mainstream Urban
Florida	Panama City	WEBZ-99.3FM	Mainstream Urban
Florida	Gainsville	WTMN-1430AM	Urban Gospel
Florida	Vero Beach/Ft.Pierce	WIRA-1400AM	Urban Gospel
Florida	Vero Beach/Ft.Pierce	WJFP-91.1FM	Urban Contemp
Florida	Vero Beach/Ft.Pierce	WFLM-104.7FM	Urban AC
Georgia	Atlanta	WPZE-102.5FM	Urban Gospel
Georgia	Atlanta	WAMJ-107.5FM	Urban AC

Georgia	Atlanta	WALR-104.1FM	Urban AC
Georgia	Atlanta	WHTA-107.9FM	Mainstream Urban
Georgia	Atlanta	WVEE-103.3FM	Urban Contemp
Georgia	Augusta	WYNF-1340AM	Urban Gospel
Georgia	Augusta	WTHB-1550AM	Urban Gospel
Georgia	Augusta	WAAW-94.7FM	Urban Gospel
Georgia	Augusta	WKSP-96.3FM	Urban AC
Georgia	Augusta	WTHB-96.9FM	Urban Gospel
Georgia	Augusta	WIIZ-97.9FM	Mainstream Urban
Georgia	Augusta	WAKB-100.9FM	Urban AC
Georgia	Augusta	WFXA-103.0FM	Mainstream Urban
Georgia	Augusta	WKZK-103.7FM	Urban Gospel
Georgia	Augusta	WPRW-107.0FM	Mainstream Urban
Georgia	Savannah	WJLG-900AM	Urban Gospel
Georgia	Savannah	WHGM-1400AM	Urban Gospel
Georgia	Savannah	WSOK-1230AM	Urban Gospel
Georgia	Savannah	WSSJ-100.1FM	Urban Gospel
Georgia	Savannah	WEAS-93.9FM	Mainstream Urban
Georgia	Savannah	WQBT-94.1FM	Mainstream Urban
Georgia	Savannah	WLVH-	Urban AC

Georgia	Savannah	101.1FM WTYB-103.9FM	Urban AC
Georgia	Columbus	WAGH-101.3FM	Urban AC
Georgia	Columbus	WBFA-98.3FM	Mainstream Urban
Georgia	Columbus	WEAM-100.7FM	Urban Gospel
Georgia	Columbus	WFXE-105.0FM	Mainstream Urban
Georgia	Columbus	WKZJ-92.7FM	Urban AC
Georgia	Macon	WFXM-107.1FM	Mainstream Urban
Georgia	Macon	WIBB-97.9FM	Mainstream Urban
Georgia	Macon	WLZN-92.3FM	Mainstream Urban
Georgia	Macon	WRBV-101.7FM	Urban AC
Georgia	Albany	WJYZ-960AM	Urban Gospel
Georgia	Albany	WJIZ-96.3FM	Mainstream Urban
Georgia	Albany	WQVE-101.7FM	Urban AC
Georgia	Albany	WMRZ-98.1FM	Urban AC
Georgia	Albany	WZBN-105.5FM	Mainstream Urban
Illinois	Chicago	WGRB-1390AM	Urban Gospel
Louisiana	New Orleans	WYLD-940AM	Urban Gospel
Louisiana	New Orleans	WPRF-94.9FM	Urban Gospel
Louisiana	Baton Rouge	WXOK-	Urban Gospel

		1460AM	
Louisiana	Shreveport/Bossier	KOKA-980AM	Urban Gospel
Louisiana	Shreveport/Bossier	KIOU-1480AM	Urban Gospel
Louisiana	Shreveport/Bossier	KSYB-1300AM	Urban Gospel
Maryland	Baltimore	WCAO-600AM	Urban Gospel
Maryland	Baltimore	WWIN-1400AM	Urban Gospel
Michigan	Detroit	WPZR-102.7FM	Urban Gospel
Michigan	Detroit	WEXL-1340AM	Urban Gospel
Michigan	Grand Rapids	WDPW-91.9FM	Urban Gospel
Washington	Seattle/Tacoma	KZIZ-1560AM	Urban Gospel
Sirius XM Radio	------------------------------	XM32	Urban Gospel
Sirius Radio	------------------------------	XS67	Urban Gospel